I AM ANGRY TODAY

**but
not
every
day**

I AM ANGRY TODAY

An original selection of poems
from the years 1990 to 2017

Peter Preston

Illuminatus Press

Peter Preston has asserted his right under the Copyright, Designs and Patents Act, 1988, to be identified as the author of this book.

First Edition printed 2017

ISBN 978-0-244-01265-6

Copyright © 2017 Peter Preston

All rights reserved. This book or any portion thereof may not be reproduced or used in any manner whatsoever without the express written permission of the publisher except for the use of brief quotations in a book review.

Published by
Illuminatus Press
Holyhead, Isle of Anglesey

PREFACE

For me, the different forms of poetry are less important than the way in which the words are revealed and created.

My poems are variously autobiographical, inspirational, aspirational, observational, or drawn from direct interaction with the subject matter.

I particularly enjoy the challenge offered by being a performance poet. And though many years of stage experience undoubtedly help with the delivery of the writing, it is the opportunity to express those words in the way that I heard them and imbue them with the subtle meanings and emphasis that arose during their creation that I find rewarding.

Offered in no particular order, the reader is invited to dip in to the selection at random.

CONTENTS

I Am Angry Today	8
The Dying of the Light	11
The Day Before You Came	12
Wife Beating	14
The Last Gateway	15
En Route to the Guillotine	16
The Plague Cart	17
Lament for a Young Mother	18
Look in the Mirror	19
Lines Written at 37,000 Feet	20
Cat's Portrait	22
Brexit Blues	24
I Love You Gwenda Hughes	26
Portmeirion	27
The Height of Service	28
Arriva Arriver	30
Prague	32
Berlin	33
Ode to Joy Once More	34
Tom's Muse	35
The Divine Undiscovered	36
A Woman of a Certain Age	38

Is This Death	41
Time Passes	42
The Boat on the Lake	43
Pyramid Planning	44
Feral Cats	45
Tea For One	46
Tell Me Sweet Heart	48
Sonnet One	49
Why Didn't You Say Something	50
Flesh in the Pan	52
Wherefore Art Thou Juliet?	54
Plastic	56
Bones of Contention	58
Don't Wait For Me	60
If Poetry Was Money	62
An Unassailable Love	64
My Father is Dead	67
Thunderstorm Spanish Style	70
Women Are Not Like Us	73
The Death of Love	76
Through a Girl's Eyes	78

I AM ANGRY TODAY

I am angry today
Angry at the passing years
Angry at lost opportunities
Angry at past mistakes

I am angry today
Angry that children think I am ancient
That ancient folk call me young man
That young people think I'm invisible

I am angry today
Angry at my inertia
For having little ambition
And accepting my fate

I am angry today
Angry that the convictions of my courage
Were often missing in action
Strewn across the battlefield of life

I am angry today
Angry that the world is sick
That the greatest force for good
Is also the most malevolent

I am angry today
Angry that my voice is too small
To stem the tide of ignorance
Rushing towards future oblivion

I am angry today
Angry at my frailty
Frustrated at my inability
To change the unchangeable

I am angry today
Angry about humanity
But mostly about inhumanity
By mankind to everything else

I am angry today
Angry that I never asked the questions
Of evaporated people
Leaving the past stuck in the past

I am angry today
Angry about the love I have wasted
And the love I have spurned
But mostly about the love I didn't notice

I am angry today
Angry in a world of broken hearts
And that along the romantic way
I should find mine and yours

I am angry today
Angry about upsetting you
And spoiling your days
You know who you are

I am angry today
Angry about politics and religion
But we don't talk about those
Because it makes me, well, you know

I am angry today
Angry about too many things
But do not remove my anger
I might get a bit annoyed by that

THE DYING OF THE LIGHT

The last days of summer
The few days of warmth
The onset of the dark
The apprehension of cold

These are the thoughts that surface
The feelings of loss

Good times put to bed
To bc wakened in spring
When the darkness recedes
And life is renewed once more

With daffodils and lambs
And girls in pretty dresses
With sunsets and swallows
And boys playing in the lane

But for now
Only in the future
A fervent hope
That the light returns

Because one day
A long time away
Far in the future
Beyond our comprehension
At a time when our star dies
Our light will too

THE DAY BEFORE YOU CAME

Life was good
I thought I was whole
Nothing left to do
The day before you came

Life was easy
I thought I was free
Nothing left to make
The day before you came

Life was relaxed
I thought I was calm
Nothing left to worry
The day before you came

Life was full
I thought I was happy
Nothing left to feel
The day before you came

Life was sweet
I thought I was done
Nothing left to earn
The day before you came

Life was a sham
I thought I was many things
Nothing left to strive for
The day before you came

Life is different
I see horizons anew
Everything to gain
The day you came

WIFE BEATING

I beat the wife the other day
Apparently it's not unlawful
In fact she got a hammering
It really was quite awful

She was beaten in the kitchen
And in the bathroom too
I showed her little mercy
As I slowly turned the screw

The neighbours don't suspect
What goes on behind our door
And I really don't suppose
That the wife can take much more

Now you might think it nasty
That I give her so much grief
But I think she really asks for it
Well, that is my belief

Today she got a thumping
But I'd like to make it clear
It had nothing to do with Class A drugs
Or whisky, gin, or beer

And tomorrow will be much the same
It's caused by her constant babble
I know what the end result will be
Cos she's not very good at Scrabble

THE LAST GATEWAY

This gateway has no empire
No space for evil forces
But fertile lawns and fragrant flowers
And courtyards of cobbles and horses

This gateway has no guardian
No troops keep foes at bay
No people crowding round its portals
Yet dogs and cats and children play

This gateway has no lock and key
No choice of passing through its door
No way of knowing what waits there
No pain is needed, any more

EN ROUTE TO THE GUILLOTINE

[Haiku]

Dark thoughts veil my sight
Unknown horror awaits me
No time for faint heart

Led by harsh rough men
Coarse rope cuts and tears my skin
Repentance is nigh

Fresh air sensed at last
How little time to breathe it
As I'm dragged upwards

The hooded man sneers
Holding an axe urgently
I avoid his eyes

The block meets my head
I hear the handle creaking
Its release also mine

THE PLAGUE CART

Cobbles rattle under our primitive transport
Its wheels turning incessantly, relentlessly
Grim horrors of being buried alive
Tear through my poisoned wretched body

Rancid and rotten terminal stenches
Fill every dying cell of my senses
I'm still alive, I silently, inwardly shout
But unhearing conspirators slumber on

Stop! Stop! I'm not dead
Let me have at least one more day
Thinking, feeling, breathing, being
Even if it is just being, just being

Mercy! Have mercy for pity's sake
But nobody hears, nobody sees
Asleep for ever, my companions stare
Wide eyed at my inevitable death

Stricken, I am tossed, seemingly lifeless
In to the deep, dark, desperate pit
Down, down, my whole life is ebbing
Slipping away with no hope of reprieve

Almost gone, a mere sliver of life remains
To remind me of life times gone by
Yet somewhere, somehow, I hope
I am not forgotten, not forsaken

LAMENT FOR A YOUNG MOTHER

O tousled sister of family of man
Who suffers life's trials as well as you can

Where do you go with that basket on wheels
With cargo that leads to more washing, more meals

You trudge in the rain with head bowed so low
Dragging wet children that don't want to know

And how can you grasp some hope in your life
When bound by your duties of mother and wife

And if you could glimpse life beyond your horizon
What sort of utopia would you set your sights on

Do your dreams seem so distant
That they are way out of reach

Are your hopes all washed up
On some far distant beach

LOOK IN THE MIRROR

Look in the mirror and what dost thou see
An image of self reflected at thee

Look at thy self and what dost thou see
The heart perhaps that yearns to be free

Look in thy heart and what dost thou feel
The love you must give and they must not steal

Look at your love, is it blessed and whole
Does it support and entwine with the soul

Look in your soul, so deep and so rare
And see the truth that all things must share

Look at the truth and live it each day
Allowing your self to walk the Great Way

Look down the Way, the Truth and the Life
And see the light that brings joy to strife

Look to the light and bathe in its glow
And so be the mirror that helped you to grow

LINES WRITTEN AT 37,000 FEET

Hushed are the people in Two Eight Nine
In contemplation of white bird's powers
Her master awaits the imminent sign
To leave from ground's controlling towers

Umbilicals severed from terra's care
Our beast of burden is released
For some it's time for silent prayer
As pulse and tension are increased

The captain turns the great white swan
And runs her engines up to speed
The pre-flight checks have all been done
So faith's with God and shining steed

With surge of power and force of G
Our Pegasus is winged aloft
More and more of Earth we see
From mercenary's block to farmer's croft

Our planet laid out far below
A large green map that comes alive
Crops to pick and lawns to mow
By city dwellers in their hive

High above the clouds we soar
A soft white bed of fleecy down
And far below an alien shore
And strange people in a foreign town

Floating on in endless space
Existence seems detached from life
One sees the universal face
And hears its music without strife

Before too long the seat belt sign
Illuminates to warn the throng
That very soon it will be time
To sing a different kind of song

With baited breath each person waits
And hopes that landing will be sure
But groundless are their doubting traits
For wheels are down and fear's no more

CAT'S PORTRAIT

An observation of a portrait of a cat painted on stone

Oh Chan, why did you have to leave
I hear your baby's cries
In my sleep
In my dreams
They call across the ether
Never leaving me
Alone
Without you

Oh, I immortalised you in stone
The stone you used to play with
On our window sill
Where you watched the goldfish
And the birds

And now I have you forever
Never ageing
Beyond the everlasting image
That stares back at me
Mirroring my feelings
Echoing my sighs
At my loss
And yours

Shall we meet again
One day
Somewhere in a new world.
I spend my time
Wondering
How it would be
If we met again

Would you know me
I would know you
The offered paw
The inclined head
The rub against my leg
Like no other

I gaze through our window
At that place
In the garden
But you are not there
Not now
Not any more

BREXIT BLUES

Brexit, Brexit, Brexit
Don't tell me about Brexit
There again perhaps you should
I wish to hell someone would

Europe Europe Europe
They shove it down our throats
And if you haven't got a clue
Brussels can tell us what to do

People People People
We've got too many you say
Or do you claim it's a mortal sin
Not to let the whole world in

Decide Decide Decide
For inertia lies in wait
Heavy is the pregnant hour
That demands your moment of power

Vote Vote Vote
Get out and make your mark
Choose to leave or stay
You might as well just pray

Remain Remain Remain
Better the devil you know
And where will the UK end
When it hasn't got a friend

Leave Leave Leave
If you want your freedom back
Then put on your running shoes
And banish those Brexit blues

Abstain Abstain Abstain
Get back on the bloody fence
Let others make your choices
And take away your voices

Result Result Result
But is it what you want
And what were you voting for
I'm sure that you're not sure

Change Change Change
Is that what we fear most
To wake up tomorrow morning
And find a different Europe dawning

I LOVE YOU GWENDA HUGHES

I love you Gwenda Hughes
With your kind face
And your flashing smile
And your bright eyes shining

I love you Gwenda Hughes
With your ham sandwiches
And your cherry cake
And your red wine flowing

I love you Gwenda Hughes
With your big breasts
And your generous hips
And your warm heart thumping

I love you Gwenda Hughes
With your short legs
And your white thighs
And your fiery furnace burning

I love you Gwenda Hughes
With your long sighs
And your contented eyes
And your whole body trembling

I love you Gwenda Hughes
With your happy hour
And your stolen moments
And your life's horizon, waiting

PORTMEIRION

[Haiku]

Peaceful, moonless night
Flowers respect the darkness
Floodlights cast shadows

Nothing seems to breathe
Secret lives remain unseen
Midnight reigns supreme

Water entertains
Fountains tinkle in dark pools
Drowning time's sweet face

Sundials are helpless
Statues stand like dead people
Waiting for dawn's light

THE HEIGHT OF SERVICE

We're flying at 38,000 feet
Or so they say
I wonder why the girls
Look prettier that way

With short cut or pony tail
Sporting a variety of styles
It's no wonder these ladies
Clock up the hair miles

With ribbons of red
And tabards of blue
They are always around
To do things for you

Was that coffee sir or beer
They will cheerfully ask
As they apply themselves readily
To each little task

A glamorous profession
It used to be said
But by a uniformed waitress
We're kept watered and fed

She parades up the aisle
So tight and so narrow
A plethora of goods
Carried on her wheeled barrow

When all's said and done
Regarding each wish
A similar trolley
Collects our rubbish

And just when we think
They have finished their shifts
They come rolling along
With perfume and gifts

Scent for the ladies
And toys for the kids
We are cutely relieved
Of residual quids

But what's this we hear
Final approach
Too late to decide
On that beautiful watch

So thank you to Charlotte
And Joanne too
For looking after us
Up in the wild blue

We won't forget Ismail
And Alan as well
They entertained all
Til the last cabin bell

ARRIVA ARRIVER

Arriva arriver, no trains no driver
No dearly departed, no passengers either

Disruption has been reported
Oh thank you very much
My journey is aborted
Whilst I wait in their hutch

They have excuses and reasons
That change with the seasons
What plausible statement will I hear them say
That attempts to justify spoiling my day

The signalling system is faulty they state
And a shortage of train crew because they are late
Plus they're blaming congestion and other tall tales
It's a wonderful service they're giving to Wales

A train's hit an obstruction on the main line
It's those engineering works not finished on time
Or the tree that's blocking the permanent way
And trespassers on the railway, earlier today

They're pleased to tell you the next train would run
If the engine hadn't failed in front of that one
And you'll only have two coaches instead of the four
As they make urgent repairs to the track once more

There's level crossing barriers refusing to lift
Train conductors not turning up for their shift
And they don't offer any sort of explanation
Why the 9.23 doesn't call at your station

There's a fault on the train so it's not coming back
And there's animals wandering the railway track
Then the next train's delayed due to slippery rails
I'll be travelling by bus if everything else fails

Arriva arriver, no trains no driver
No dearly departed, no passengers either

PRAGUE

Riding the Orient Express
    up the winding Elba valley
Walking across the Charles Bridge
    thick with foreign tongues
Riding the Russian metro
    in the perpetual rush hour
Strolling the Mala Strana
    hearing the Kafka echoes
Walking the streets of grandeur
    and breathing in the history
Eating in the courtyards
    of unchanged buildings
Drinking in the bars
    where politicians deceived
Soaking up the feeling
    of an ambition achieved

BERLIN

Cruising the Berlin autobahn
    and stopping for coffee
Driving through the city traffic
    wishing I was elsewhere
Staying in old East Berlin
    evoking old memories
Walking in the Tiergarten
    enjoying the last of summer
Sitting in the sky drawing
    circles in the Radio Tower
Walking in the shadow
    of the Brandenburg Gate
Cruising down the river
    past the last of the Wall
Thinking of my journeys
    And where next to call

ODE TO JOY ONCE MORE

Joy came in to my life
Though that wasn't her name
She had fire in her hair
And her face fanned a flame

She had not come alone
There was baggage and things
The hesitance of discovery
And family and rings

But boldly she strode
And crossed the divide
With a firmness of purpose
To be by my side

For now we are sharing
And walk the Great Way
Discovering each other
Each blessed new day

TOM'S MUSE

I wish that life was easy and not so complicated
Spending all this time rushing round getting mated
For though I get the pleasure of eyeing up the birds
It would seem rather fun if it wasn't so absurd

I already have all that one could require
A home, a family, a nice warm fire
So what else could one possibly need
Unless it had to do with selfishness and greed

Of course I like a little fun
Lazing around in the noonday sun
But I still keep my secrets deep
For I'm not too fussy where I sleep

And I always seem to be having fights
And waging wars with parasites
Always competing with the human race
To keep my hard fought living space

All the same, on a cold winter's day
When man must go out to earn his pay
I just stay at home, getting fat
You see I am, after all, a cat

THE DIVINE UNDISCOVERED

I see thee from a distance
A special being as yet unfurled
Waiting for a discovery
That is yet to be made

What is this special power
That holds me in check
Awaiting the burst of reasoning
That defies reason

Shall I find that ending
That untold story
That mystery that beckons
If only in my mind

Shall spirits separate us
In this lifetime that boundaries
Distant from the affliction
Imagined in my psyche

Perhaps spirits do not decree
That conjunction be enjoined
In this never ending spiral
Of life's eternal journey

Shall we never meet
This life's undying meeting
Never forge the promise
Of a duty not envisaged

When will this torment
Find a form
That once endangered
Never more engages

Shall I live in peace
Or death with this emotion
A secret that scarcely promised
Presses deep within my need

I dare not find expression
A certainty of emotion
Which rests in God's lap
Waiting for a found ending

A WOMAN OF A CERTAIN AGE

She is near
But afar
Her presence omni present
Her welcome all encompassing

Yet giving without asking
She risks contentment
Investing time in affection
Devoting spiritual energy
And an endearing intimacy
A selfless offering of kindness
And tenderness of the soul

The domain of her heart
Guarded yet available
Impenetrable yet accessible
It is all things to all men
But not to be taken lightly
In the autumn days
Of life's various journeys

The past a long lost country
The future an unknown land
The present lies scattered
In the fields of blurred reality

She is a refuge for sentiment
A harbour for aged romance
A sanctuary for love
A haven for passion
An asylum for the madness
Of expedient flirtation

A woman of understanding
Considerate of weakness
Forgiving of infirmity
Tolerant of imperfection

Our flaws and frailties
Our shared impediments
Are all grist to the mill
All just slings and arrows
To be born gladly
In defence of the realm
Of outrageous union

The Villanelle

A French verse form consisting of five three-line stanzas and a final quatrain, with the first and third lines of the first stanza repeating alternately in the following stanzas. These two refrain lines form the final couplet in the quatrain.

See "Do Not Go Gentle into That Good Night" by Dylan Thomas, Elizabeth Bishop's "One Art," and Edwin Arlington Robinson's "The House on the Hill."

This Villanelle in 8 "Is This Death" was dedicated to the funeral of my friend, the shaman Dei Hughes.

IS THIS DEATH?

Oh tell me death where is thy sting
That final bite at closing time
And then thy praises I may sing

And is there one more final fling
One last great hill that I must climb
Oh tell me death where is thy sting

I'll not be here to see the spring
So let me make just one more rhyme
And then thy praises I may sing

Though no more children's voices sing
No more the scent of sage and thyme
Oh tell me death where is thy sting

So let me come and join the Ring
Then walk your stage in silent mime
And then thy praises I may sing

Now face to face I see the King
And angel's faces quite sublime
Oh tell me death where is thy sting
And then thy praises I may sing

TIME PASSES

Time passes but slowly
For a love left to smoulder
Space to mature
Before it gets older
Room to strengthen
Afore it gets bolder
A test of the heart
To ensure it's no colder
If love needs a surety
We'll be its holder
In times of sadness
Seek out my shoulder
For my lady weeps softly
And I wait patient to hold her

THE BOAT ON THE LAKE

Far across the lake my boat there lay
Shorn of its rigging and lost its way
Could I rescue my dear old vessel
From the weeds in which it did nestle

Separated from rusty hulk
One had to choose twixt plan or sulk
The sad sight of my distant wreck
Showed tilted and haphazard deck

With courage plucked at last I waded
In terms of help alas unaided
With no compass or sextant to hand
My longitude lay not on dry land

Heading out across the waters deep
A stormy rendezvous I did keep
My lifeless boat I did bravely save
And rescued it from a watery grave

With happy step and growing pride
Having mastered strong wind and tide
A resolute and resourceful boy
Drifted home with his salvaged toy

Author's Note
Being an exercise in alliterative poetry where each line is constrained to have three words beginning with the same letter or sound.

PYRAMID PLANNING

Masons meandered amongst the marble
Preparing plans on laundered parchment

Slaves strained on ropes and strings
Perfect pyramids in preparation

Saintly sarcophagi waited sagely
Never knowing daytime from night

Failed Pharaohs prematurely fallen
Were wistfully readied by the wise

Tragic teenage Tutankhamun
Kept from kingship by karmic death

Inscribed incantations inimitably carved
Lives legibly recorded in lasting precision

Mummies mortal remains in modernity
Now microscopically murdered in museums

Carter's curse their own conclusion
Torn from tombs to tantalise scholars

FERAL CATS

[Haiku]

Courtship powers wane
The young cats perform best
Just memories left

The big light has gone
Distant views are meaningless
Just lamps in the sky

Food and warmth are prime
A hunt for something precious
The need for fullness

The howling is spent
Moonshine lights the dismal sea
Another day ends

Vital signs are weak
Breath comes uneasily
Morning is welcome

TEA FOR ONE

An empty room
A cold teapot
No more the cry goes up
How about a nice cup of tea

No more bacon and eggs
Swimming in fat
Because she didn't see too well
Vanity is a terrible thing

Now there are just stains
Blood, food and other things
On the carpet
Proving the survival of bodily fluids
After death

Now she looks down upon us all
Not just the neighbours
Her disdain for people
Finally extinguished

Look after your mother when I'm gone
Said my father
And he quietly went
And we solemnly did

Until the day of the phone call
Your mother has passed away
Said a voice from the home
With rehearsed compassion

I was in Manchester
On my way to Old Trafford
She was in Caernarfon
Going nowhere

I saw the cricket through
And kissed her goodbye the next day
Our family is like that

TELL ME SWEET HEART

Tell me sweet heart from whence the fire rises
That burns my breast with strong fire of love
For the turbulent emotion that moves beneath me
Waits patient for time to swell forth above

Who is it, this smouldering mortal that lives
If only to escort this expression of joy
And aspires to hear the voice of his dreams
And gaze upon his Helen of Troy

And when this man beholds his Venus
His heart in tumult, so much to tell
He wonders if she shares his passion
His wish for both to hear the same bell

And what wondrous dream do this pair conjure
In this unyielding world where all men fail
Perhaps just for triumph over disaster
Whilst on the quest for their personal grail

So what path to tread in times to come
What choice to make when stars align
Which instincts to follow when love is calling
When hearts eternal strings entwine

SONNET ONE

A Sonnet in memory of Dei Hughes
30th January 2004

Love's door is never barred on grounds of age
A life of many days can show its worth
Hearts young on earth may choose the wizened sage
Though many years divide their time of birth
For time itself sits on the side of those
Whose mortal journey pass the half way mark
For they shall have no urgency to close
The gate on nature's basic human spark
Tis not the custom that we now pretend
That a secret love knot doth not endure
Indeed, display is made to make amend
For cupid's sickness hath no simple cure
Though pale faced youth hath long since rung his bell
The wrinkled master still has tale to tell

WHY DIDN'T YOU SAY SOMETHING

You kept your secret for sixty years
Why didn't you say something

We would have understood
We would have understood you
Understood why things were the way they were

You denied us the right to have a sister
Dismissed your own child to hide the pain
The poor child had to die twice
To help you through the hurt
Why didn't you say something

Finding Angela lifeless in her pram
Only three months allowed for love
You carried a lifeless shell for a mile
Through unknowing London streets
Why didn't you say something

We all paid for this loss of life
It cost you some of your sanity
It cost me some of my childhood
And my brother was culpable

His needs distracted you long enough
His sister's silent urgency went unheeded
And his detached part was never forgotten
And I wasn't born a girl
The replacement that never was
Why didn't you say something

The years passed in secret
An invisible dread hanging forever
Over a strange tacit event
Never to be spoken of
Never to be documented
Why didn't you say something

Until that bizarre day of rebirth
And the realisation of re-death
The uncovering of a long hidden life
And it was too late to ask you
Long past the time for sharing
Why didn't you say something

But you didn't take your secret
To the grave
I couldn't allow that
I mentioned her name once
And in that deep dark soul of senility
You knew that I knew
And you went back behind the veil
Why didn't you say something

FLESH IN THE PAN

Christmas is coming
And the goose is getting fat
It's no concern of mine
That he's got as fat as that
And turkeys, ducks and quadrupeds
Would safely sleep within their beds
If the world was vegetarian

Our television ads run red with blood
From benign bovines that never made stud
One mourns dead creatures
In the butchers I pass
To them I will not raise
A stiff festive glass
Not from where I'm standing

If you must eat meat go out and kill it
Then we'll see what's on your skillet
Arm yourself with gun and knife
Go out in the country and take a life
And then it's personal

The anonymous flesh
Lying on your plate
That has kept an involuntary December date
Once roamed the fields
And shared your air
Now only you can stand and stare
At what you've done

So go and make your carnivorous choice
Deny living creatures their life and voice
But remember they once had faces and feelings
But could not resist hypocritical dealings
Dare to share their tears

When your table is laden with Christmas un-fayre
Spare some time to lay your conscience bare
And ignoring celebrations twixt floor and rafter
Decide if you're part of man's slaughter
Or man's laughter
And live with it

WHEREFORE ART THOU JULIET?

Wherefore art thou Juliet?
I love thee but I do not know thee
The contrast of emotions
Startling in its proportion

I wait for thee to appear
Thy balcony doth display nothing
I fear thou sleepest beyond my call
My love waits patient for audience

Time standeth still
Waiting uponst any urgency
Thy apparition resists all call
Thy appearance disdains all desire

Wherefore art thou my Juliet?
For though that be thy name
This undeniable urge renames thee
Protects thy real self from purge

I yearn for that which thou bearest
And hunt the elusive breast of love
Worship the ground that thou walks upon
And desires only the best for our unity

I care not what the world thinks
Dismiss all words opposeth to thee
All I see is thy smile shining
All I want is for love to be free

I will wait eternally for thee
Even though my quiet voice is nigh
In tears, I hope that thou hears it
That one day you will hear me pass by

PLASTIC

Getting old really sucks
She said
With feeling
Her words emerging invisibly
From under the thatch
Of someone else's hair

That profound statement
Said in all innocence
There being no evidence
The uttered words were hers

A face with no expression
A mouth frozen in time
Her skin torn from a drum
And rehomed without shame

Seventy going on thirty
Hawking ageing wares
Expensively disguised
By a life of graft

Her life a constant struggle
Against unrelenting years
Preserving a history
Of constructed beauty

Her looks in grave danger
Always on the brink of collapse
Having to save face
At the point of a knife

A surgeon's butchery
The only protection
Against ravages of time
Undesirable fat
Superfluous lines
The steady march south

That regular scenario
Constantly repeated
A suffocating cycle
Of despair and repair
With eternal respite
Only beyond death's door

BONES OF CONTENTION

I have a black satanic friend
Always there when you don't need him
No king had a more loyal subject
No doctor had a more persistent patient

This infernal incessant worm
Feeding hungrily on my infirmity
Constantly disrespectful of age
Vengeful and spiteful without reason

He declares war on my peace
Assaults my joi de vivre
Intrudes upon my private moment
And interrupts my deepest thinking

Subtle as a siege gun
He ploughs my settled furrow
Scattering seeds of resentment
Rejoicing in the harvest of my pain

Impotent against this invisible bully
I shake my hand at an internal enemy
For to shake my fist would defeat the object
And increase the power of the master

He arrives from out of nowhere
The ever unwelcome guest
Long outstaying his welcome
Selfishly setting his own agenda

My mean spirited visitor
Explores my skeletal frailty
Cloaking his force of evil
Crushing medicinal defences

An undesirable companion
I await his next sinuous engagement
Earnestly enjoying his absence
In a life of bony trepidation

This malevolent masked creature
An invisible personal highwayman
Stands in wait at bodily crossroads
Whilst I accept the inevitable deliverance

DON'T WAIT FOR ME

Don't wait for me as I won't be there
It might not have been an intention
In the present incarnation of cosmic dust
To be captured by the certainty of change

Don't wait for me as I won't be there
I might be far away doing good things
Or close by doing performing bad deeds
Sowing seeds is a constant game of chance

Don't wait for me as I won't be there
So don't waste time on hope and trust
Time and tide still wait for no man
They certainly will not wait for me

Don't wait for me as I won't be there
There again it's not a promise made
Who knows where one might be standing
In a world of cruel uncertain action

Don't wait for me as I won't be there
You can be at heaven's gate if you like
If that's what takes your secular fancy
If that's where your belief takes you

Don't wait for me as I won't be there
You might arrive there before me
You might turn up after the event
And I might never appear to be seen

Don't wait for me as I won't be there
Not in any normal physical sense
Only you can make me attend the moment
Using memory as your crutch of support

Don't wait for me as I won't be there
But you will wait for ever and ever
Until you grow weary of the waiting
And hope that people will wait for you

IF POETRY WAS MONEY

If poetry was money
And one could float alone
In a sea of desperate scribes
Then a writer of note
Could coin a phrase
And make a treasury of work

Would romantic poetry
Be legally tender
And altruism
A verse to wealth
Would desire overcome truth
Creating canon fodder

Would a line of credit
End at a point
Of no return
Would your word
No longer
Be your bond

Would you profit
From the mistakes
Of forged text
Or be called to account
For illicit earnings
And outrageous fortune

Would one strike a balance
Between honest originality
And riches beyond avarice
Or leave the debt to society
Letting the burden of gilts
Taint your precious mettle

Would a thread of silver
Run through your work
Or would the glister of gold
Tarnish your rewards
And literary consideration
Be subservient to greed

But if the crowd passes by
Ere your ink is dry
Would art be deranged
To see currency exchanged
Would one churn out trash
To accumulate cash

AN UNASSAILABLE LOVE

I care not what they think
They can all go to hell
I care only what she thinks
How her opinion matters to me

I am misled by people of no consequence
Disturbed by those of personal desire
But my lover and her dedication
Are the arrows to my bow of life's conclusion

Why seek farther than what I have
Why check the grass on the other side
It is the fence that remains crucial
That divides the external from my abide

The intrinsic value of our love
Has no worth beyond our own appreciation
Cannot respond to external influence
Offers no purchasing power to potential buyers

A lattice of contentment settles over me
Constrains my idle thoughts and sentiments
Restrains my wilder pathetic instincts
And controls my senseless urges

I look at my self in isolation
Resplendent in worthless self esteem
My judgement rests in the hands of others
With those with values above mine own

Respecting love as an institution
Rejecting marriage as an acceptable face
One ever remembers the dedication
Resting in the hands of detached love

Never forgetting that she is there
Silently supporting thy worthless endeavours
She only desires the shared ambition
That contentment ultimately delivers unhindered

I sometimes see her knitting or writing
Astounded at the dedication of skilled hands
Watching as art appears from nowhere
Witnessing the results of unappreciated hours

I worship the ground she walks upon
As I do for all sentient creatures
But her pasture is where you will find me
Choosing a glimpse of her forbidden land

Nothing will stop me from loving her
And all else that moves and breathes
She stands out worthy of consequence
Demanding my primary attention

So I rest my case of commitment
Offer no defence of existence
My lance of perpetual engagement
Is offered uncontrollably to thee

MY FATHER IS DEAD

My father is dead
Long live my father
I see his face in my mind
Still feel the fear at his return

I peer through cracks in time
Wincing at harsh discipline
I reach out to him in declining years
And find an equality of manhood

I wonder if he sees what I feel
Parenting years given to hard work
Dropping in as an occasional visitor
The migratory feeder of his young

Working most of the hours God sends
And my later life follows suit
The inheritance of his work ethic
Branded indelibly upon my hide

Not knowing I was supposed to love him
Put off by the hard hand of correction
His footfall that of the schoolmaster
Scolding me in advance of our meeting

Wait til your father gets home
Mother would say with earnest conviction
And I would repair to my room
Awaiting the call to furious arms

Time passes as the house falls quiet
Gradually the threat fades away
Was my crime unworthy of punishment
Or was I under maternal protection

Looking back on such episodes
I come to a tacit understanding
That mother's incapacity to cope
Balanced her inability to restrain

Relentless years passed by
And visited upon by parenthood
That melee of blessing and curse
Fell upon me with disproportionate clarity

I look back on our shared moments of maturity
Incredibly I'm allowed to drive his beloved car
And stand next to him on the cricket field
Held up as the result of his reproduction

Fifteen years of welcome retirement
Educate the gaps in our lives
Revelations punctuate our reunions
As we discover our mutual selves

Dutiful terminal painful years follow
The last conversation already a memory
We no longer hear each other's voices
As the inevitable waiting game plays out

Now motionless he lies before me
His life force permanently spent
And unable to hear my last farewell
I can only imagine his spiritual reply

My father is no longer alive
His death also partly mine own
The release from his suffering most welcome
As I witness his last journey alone

THUNDERSTORM SPANISH STYLE

High up in the Sierra Nevada
They are whispering
The meek of the earth
Feel the vibrations of change
And prepare to welcome
The onslaught of nature

Little feet scurry to safe harbour
Grassing up the oncoming storm
To fellows of their kind
Passing up the food chain
The impending deluge
Is soon news to all creatures

Demonic clouds gather their strength
Precursors to thunder that drowns all else
Yet no watery deliverance is evident
As day turns in to night
The air grows colder
And the atmosphere is electric

Then all goes terrifyingly silent
The trees are nodding
Their fear being one of dryness
Quite opposite to the animals
That crouch and worry
Under the desperate branches

All expectations are satisfied
Raindrops begin to splatter
Pea sized watery spheres
Dispensing large dark circles
Upon the parched landscape
Harbingers of doom to hasty shelters

All at once the heavens open
New rivers form instantly
Regular rhythmic thunderclaps
Reinforcing apprenticed rumbles
Announce the arrival of water
In volumes fit to terrify

Lightning severs the sky
Adding harsh reality
To the son et lumière
As earth's wild audience
Fumbles for its latchkey
Clinging to proverbial life

This biblical rain
With force almost spent
Gives way to greater danger
Hailstones crash to the ground
Like machine gun bullets
Hitting forever unwary targets

Tiny species run for refuge
The prospect of imminent drowning
Replaced by risk of terminal impact
Their sole dedicated ambition
To squat wherever they can
And ride out the indiscriminate storm

Their patience finally rewarded
The air humanely dries
And as the ground gives vent to evaporation
They hear the plants give shoots of thanks
And tremulously first footing a brave new world
They step out with all recent memory washed clean

WOMEN ARE NOT LIKE US

A woman is a strange thing
She can be all things to all men
Yet nothing to her own self
A multitude of sentient beings

She may be lost in the labyrinth of love
Yet blinded by the honesty of hate
Cut open by knives of jealousy
Softened by the touch of a child

She has a confusing mixture of directions
Yet a pointed directness beyond all change
Her eyes focused on divine existence
She still sees the most basic need

Afar she hears a cry for help
The decision to answer the call
Made without final rational thought
Her response instinctive beyond distraction

A woman may be relied upon to do something
We are not always in a place of knowing
Privileged to understand its reason
Our duty is to accept its execution

A young woman lords it with her power
A lady shares it with her competitors
But the mature female grasps the moment
And achieves the impossible in a heartbeat

A woman has unreachably beautiful facets
Each facing its own transcendent futures
We know not how to view them
How to appreciate their lucidity

We are slaves to these creatures of torment
Bound by their ability to be right
They elude our attempts to translate them
And shut off our attempts to delight

We climb the gendered cliff to reach them
Belay our thoughts to their perfumed summit
Ever failing in the emotional traverse
Marooned at the base camp of masculinity

Our best hope is one of acceptance
And respecting the anointed sex
We submit to their superior aspirations
And bow down to inevitable submission

Women are not like any of our gender
They own a love beyond our comprehension
Exposed as strange beings from our viewpoint
But they will never be as strange as men

THE DEATH OF LOVE

I am torn from my reverie
Released from a blinding desire
Dismissed from the flame of service
Shackled in a well of loneliness

I reach out to touch the invisible
Aware that my quest has no home
The only eyes and ears that respond
Are the senses of my inner weeping

I am blessed with a tidal wave of tears
Yet never enough to wash my sorrow clean
I exist if only for my own sake
Breathe merely to extend my pain

I step back awhile from the mist
The shadow I see is not mine
A brutal force of rejection
Stands staring at my helpless form

A witness to the splitting of our atoms
It offers no clues to redemption
Refuses to point me in a direction
Where salvation will find me alone

I understand this lonely battle
But not the reason or the cause
My inner demons fight on
And I am divorced from their war

Time will heal most personal wounds
The pendulum of life will swing interminably
My blood will continue its mortal journey
In a bid to refresh the arteries of emotion

I stand convicted of undying grief
My only judge is my lonely heart
It sends me down to darker passages
As I am imprisoned in the death of love

THROUGH A GIRL'S EYES

She sits before me
A lady of infinite years
And unknown summers
And unspoken winters

I look in her eyes
And see the young girl
With pigtail then pony tail
Just another pretty girl perhaps

I search deeper behind the eyes
See the teenage adventuress
Reins still held tight
By caring parental control

She knows I am there
Cannot see me watching
Curious at my presence
Fearful of my maturity

I yearn for her youth
And mourning its passing
Reach out to its joy
Hang on to its ephemeral quality

Unable to see clearly
I imagine her face
It is pure and unburdened
And only has eyes for today

I think I am in love
For to be in love
Is an eternally safe place
Along the road to perfection

The lady I see now
Retains that face of clarity
Remembers the formative years
And gently smiles at their innocence

Her face exudes eternal youth
Undimmed by decades of experience
She flirts amongst trusted company
Dares to share her valued memories

Her beauty is more than skin deep
The mirror deceives her reality
Her revulsion at its reflection
Unconfirmed by all else except her

And now she is beyond years
We meet on level ground
Now she understands me
Knows that I know that she knows

My spiritual desire wants to reach out
To delicately touch her outer being
Using a loving passport
Of uninvited tenderness and care

But to try and contact her inner being
One would have to risk everything
Throw one's hat in to the eternal ring of life
To experience a precious moment of her life's time

I look again at eyes unchanged
Discerning more clearly things seen before
They look back at me with female precision
A gaze of welcome and permission endures

My exalted privilege is beyond words
She knows my story awaits her trust
I penetrate this lady's eyes in depth
And all I see are the eyes of a young girl

ACKNOWLEDGEMENT

I would like to thank the South Wales poet Patrick Jones for giving me the inspiration and courage to start performing my poetry to an audience. Some years ago, I spent an evening at the launch of one of his books and this is where I became truly aware of the satisfaction that writers can get from performing their own work.

WEBSITES

https://sites.google.com/site/ucheldrerepertorycompany/

https://sites.google.com/site/pakalaproductions/

CONTACT THE AUTHOR

Peter may be contacted via the Contact page on his Ucheldre Repertory Company website above.